NATURE'S EXTREMES

LAWRENCE W. CHEEK

EIGHT SEASONS SHAPE A SOUTHWESTERN LAND

ARIZONA HIGHWAYS
BOOKS

ACKNOWLEDGMENTS

Many people generously helped contribute to this book with their experiences, insights, and science. Many thanks are due to Mark Dimmitt of the Arizona-Sonora Desert Museum; Steve Yoder of The Arboretum at Flagstaff; Tim Grier, Curt Gustafson, Sjors Horstman, Doug Kreutz, and Nicky Leach.

COLORFUL WEBSITES

The Arizona-Sonora Desert Museum maintains an excellent website with a large section on wildflowers: www.desertmuseum.org.

Each fall The Arboretum at Flagstaff provides updates as autumn color breaks out in the Flagstaff-Oak Creek Canyon forests: www.thearb.org.

PHOTOGRAPHY CREDITS

Front Cover, left to right, Randy Prentice, George Stocking, David Muench, George Stocking, Steve Bruno, David Muench, Jack Dykinga, Jack Dykinga

Tom Bean, 76

Nick Berezenko, 31, 128

Paul and Shirley Berquist, 14, 45, 60

Steve Bruno, 96

Robert Campbell, 42, 100

Bob Clemenz, 128-129

Bruce Clendenning, 104

Michael Collier, 138

Tom Danielsen, 44-45, 141, 146-147

Larry Dech, 59

Dick Dietrich, 124-125, 137

Jack Dykinga, 18, 19, 25, 29, 33, 47, 53, 54, 58, 60-61, 62-63, 63, 64, 66, 66-67, 68-69, 69, 70-71, 72, 91, 97, 114, 117, 130, 148, 150

Jim Honcoop, 59

George H. H. Huey, 136

Gary Ladd, 55, 73, 104-105, 109, 110, 111, 113

Chuck Lawsen, 6-7, 42-43, 127, 139

David W. Lazaroff, 16, 145

Larry Lindahl, 26-27, 27, 154-155

Les Manevitz, 158-159

Robert G. McDonald, 46, 52, 82-83, 86, 118-119, 126-127, 135, 140

Morey K. Milbradt, 20-21

David Muench, 4, 8-9, 12-13, 14-15, 32, 34, 36-37, 37, 49, 50-51, 112, 131, 133, 151, 153

Marc Muench, 158

Randy Prentice, 11, 30, 34-35, 38, 38-39, 50, 65, 84-85, 98-99, 99, 115, 116, 120, 157

Jerry Sieve, 28, 144, 146, 149, 152

George Stocking, 2-3, 48, 80, 81, 85, 87, 90, 92-93, 101, 103, 134

William Stone, 94, 102

Tom Story, 77, 78, 79, 82

Tom Till, 156, 160

Richard K. Webb, 121

Frank Zullo, 17

Back Cover, Marty Cordano

A kaleidoscope of all that was wonderful, weird, terrible, and awe-inspiring: A montage of photograph details (front cover) from each chapter represents the author's concept of eight Arizona seasons.

Lyrical descriptions by author John C. Van Dyke began to change America's view of the desert as a drab, hostile place: Stately saguaros (right) grow on a *bajada,* or alluvial slopes, spreading from the base of Four Peaks in the Mazatzal Mountains east of Phoenix.

GEORGE STOCKING

Arizona's climate is too extravagant and too moody to stuff into the convenient niches of spring, summer, fall, and winter: The sun riding low in a cloudy sky (left) converts a common scene into a dramatic one in the Santa Catalina Mountains north of Tucson.

Contents

Book Designer: MARY WINKELMAN VELGOS
Photography Editor: RICHARD MAACK
Copy Editor: EVELYN HOWELL
Book Editor: BOB ALBANO

Prepared by the Book Division of *Arizona Highways*® magazine, a monthly publication of the Arizona Department of Transportation.

Publisher: Nina M. La France / Managing Editor: Bob Albano / Associate Editor: Evelyn Howell
Art Director: Mary Winkelman Velgos / Photography Director: Peter Ensenberger
Production Director: Cindy Mackey

*Arizona's dramatic climate has created the land's dramatic
natural beauty. It's that simple:* A summer storm pounds
the Bradshaw Mountains south of Prescott.

Introduction

Savage and Tender

. . . Not only purgatory and hell, but heaven likewise, had combined to produce a bewildering kaleidoscope of all that was wonderful, weird, terrible, and awe-inspiring, with not a little that was beautiful and romantic.

— John G. Bourke,
On the Border With Crook, 1891

IT IS THE PERFECT SUMMER DAY — 108° and promising.

Doug Kreutz and I, reporters at Tucson's afternoon newspaper, are rolling out to lunch in my Fiat roadster. We peel back the top for maximum ventilation and — go figure — dine on incendiary green chile at South Tucson's primo Mexican restaurant. Returning to the office, stuffed with enchilada cheer, we notice a puffy, gray-white cumulonimbus bank massing over the Santa Rita Mountains, 30 miles to the south. We debate briefly. It's been months since the last rain. No one would miss us. And so we speed south on Interstate 19, two 35-year-olds playing hooky.

The temperature edges down, maybe to a cool 100°, as we begin driving up an incline into Madera Canyon, a piney cleft in the northwestern slope of the Santa Ritas. The heavily drooping sky, its lumpy clouds now a gunmetal color, begins churning and boiling. We stop to build the Fiat's flimsy canvas top. Doug asks how much protection it might offer in the event of a lightning strike. I had re-cently asked an electrical engineer that exact question, and I relay his confident answer: "Almost none."

The rain begins to fall in wide, fat drops, thudding on the ragtop. We surge up the canyon, the tires seeming to slurp the moisture in joy. It's been a long time for them, too. Lightning crashes. The shower turns into a torrent.

We hit the end of the road and park, facing south into the teeth of the storm. Nobody else is out here; people apparently think it's a bad day. The storm hammers our Italian tent with furious Arizona fists, and amazingly it holds. Doug and I stare through the windshield, listening, looking, not talk-ing. Instinctively, we are absorbing the storm's energy, the life-giving emotional transfusion of the rain.

We return to the newsroom at 4 o'clock. It's empty. Final edition was stuffed into bed three hours ago. Doug, suffering a small in-ternal storm of guilt over taking an unautho-rized afternoon off, sits down and writes a fine essay about taking an unauthorized af-ternoon off. I mull the afternoon's events for 20 years and write a book. We prove again what Arizonans have understood for cen-turies, even millennia: The sky overhead may appear lovely or violent, or any gradation be-tween, but always it has the power to amaze and inspire.

ARIZONA'S dramatic climate has created the land's dramatic natural beauty. It's that simple.

See the skeleton of a long-dead but still-standing saguaro bleaching in the summer sun, spraying its ribs into the sky with the grace of a Roman fountain, and thank the aridity that preserves it in place.

Stand on the lip of the Grand Canyon and wonder how that piddling river could have carved such a titanic sculpture, and be informed that it didn't: It had plenty of help. Flash floods carried abrasive debris in season-al torrents, scouring channels with prehis-toric Brillo pads. Rainwater collected in

The sky always has the power to amaze and inspire: The Sonoran Desert (pages 8-9) basks in sunshine while a rainbow signals the end of a storm over the Santa Rita Mountains south of Tucson.

See the skeleton of a saguaro and thank the aridity that preserves it: A saguaro skeleton (right), seeming to be the work of a sculptor, continues providing a home for desert creatures.

RANDY PRENTICE

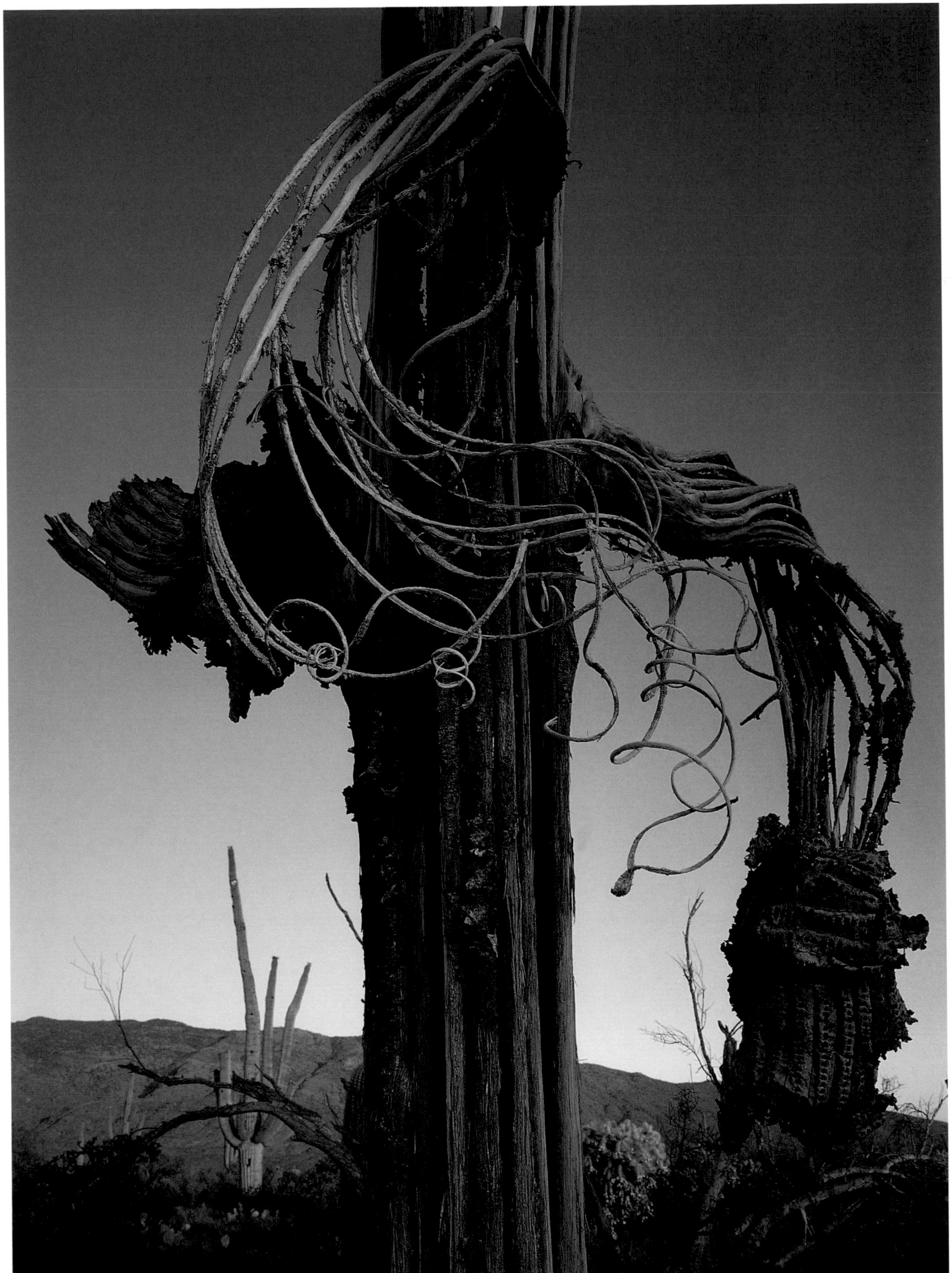

fissures, freezing and expanding, splitting off grand chunks of rock. Thank the diurnal checkerboard of hot days and cold nights.

Stumble across (not literally, please) a Gila monster during an April hike, and understand that the spring warmth has triggered its cashew-sized reptile brain to release urgent sex hormones, so our Sonoran Desert landscape is enriched by foot-long orange-and-black lizards foraging for mates.

In good years, spring splatters a frenzy of wildflowers across the deserts — poppies the color of oranges, sand verbenas that seem to blend into the sunsets, penstemons that form orchestras of miniature fuchsia trumpets. Then in other years, fickle as the weather, the land offers all the color of a pile of khaki uniforms awaiting the laundry. But such drabness makes the maniacally colorful seasons all the more precious, reminding us of the earth's endless capacity for change and surprise.

In every year, fall brings color from other than the obvious plant sources. Afternoon

How could the river carve out such a titanic place, an observer might wonder: The Grand Canyon (left) evolved over eons from the combined efforts of the Colorado River, floods raging off the Colorado Plateau, and other natural elements.

breezes stir up the Colorado Plateau's fine, red dust into an atmospheric filter, turning the late sunlight into an ocher varnish. The sunlight washes over brilliant yellow cotton-woods on canyon floors, highlighting them against salmon-colored sandstone canyon walls. In this scene, the seasonal elements align themselves just as needed for a miracle, a miracle that the ancient Navajo Night Chant speaks of as "the house made of the evening twilight."

Arizona's landscape offers us houses made of twilight and of countless elements of Nature. Some, like the wildflowers and the turning of the cottonwoods, are easy to see and celebrate. For others, we must coax our senses to appreciate their eccentric beauty.

AS LONG as there has been a written lan-guage at hand, Arizonans and itinerant visi-tors have recorded strong and sometimes colorful feelings about the extravagances of this climate. Father Ignaz Pfefferkorn, a German Jesuit missionary who spent 11 years in the Sonoran Desert beginning in 1756, was shocked by its violent extremes, even though he praised it as "altogether a blessed country." Of the daily summer rains, he wrote:

> [They] would surely be considered as priceless blessings of nature were they not always accompanied by the most horrible thunder-storms, which not infrequently do great damage to men and animals in the villages and in the fields. One cannot listen to the continuous crashing of the thunder without shuddering.

Asthmatic New Jersey art professor John C. Van Dyke wandered the Southwestern deserts from 1898 to 1901 and chronicled beauty everywhere he looked. His slim clas-sic, *The Desert* (1901), began reversing America's view of the region as a drab waste-land. Van Dyke reveled even in the "scarves of heat" rising "upon the opalescent wings of the mirage" and the "reek of color" in the sunsets. He spent days staring into what most

In good years, spring splatters a frenzy of wildflowers across the deserts: Poppies (right) decorate a meadow in the Coyote Mountains on the Tohono O'Odham Reservation west of Tucson. A Gila monster (above) prowls the spring desert for a mate.

of us still would see as a featureless sky, just bathing in its utter blueness: "[It] is beautiful in itself and merely as color. It is not necessary that it should mean anything. . . . There is no tale or text or testimony to be tortured out of the blue sky. It is a splendid body of color; no more."

Van Dyke, however, was ahead of his time. Most travelers to the Southwest were inclined to celebrate the seasons as Charles Phelps did in 1882 with a rather ineptly rhymed poem titled *Yuma*:

> Weary, weary, desolate,
> Sand-swept, parched, and cursed of fate;
> Burning, but how passionless!
> Barren, bald, and pitiless!
>
> Through all ages baleful moons
> Glared upon thy whited dunes;

And malignant, wrathful suns
Fiercely drank thy streamless runs.

Two developments rehabilitated Arizona's climate in the eyes of the people who were streaming in to stay as permanent residents. The obvious one was air conditioning, beginning with evaporative systems, or "swamp coolers," in the 1930s, followed by the quick spread of refrigeration in the 1950s and 1960s. By 1940, Phoenix led the nation in the number of air-conditioned homes, and a prominent local builder, Del Webb, probably spoke for everybody when he said it "has enabled Phoenix to meet and conquer the summer heat, long the bane of southwestern existence." In order for us to fully appreciate winter, something had to dismantle the dread of summer.

The other change embodies an attitude rather than a physical object. The transformation started with the environmental movement in the 1970s and bloomed with the rapid growth of hiking, mountain biking, river running, and outdoor sports of all kinds. To fully participate in Nature, to be *of* this earth, not just *on* it, you take her exactly as she comes — baleful moons and whited dunes along with the purple mountain majesties. Edward Abbey showed the way in his 1968 *Desert Solitaire,* the brilliant delinquent grandson of *The Desert*:

> Noontime here is like a drug. The light is psychedelic, the dry electric air narcotic. To me the desert is stimulating, exciting, exacting; I feel no temptation to sleep or to relax into occult dreams but rather an opposite effect which sharpens and heightens vision, touch, hearing, taste

Summer rains, a Jesuit missionary wrote, "would surely be considered as priceless blessings of nature were they not always accompanied by the most horrible thunderstorms:" A sunset's glorious colors (left) can mask the intensity of a storm. Lightning (above) cuts a pattern in a gray sky, creating an artistic sight as well as a danger for people and animals.

JACK DYKINGA

and smell. Each stone, each plant, each grain of sand exists in and for itself with a clarity that is undimmed by any suggestion of a different realm. *Claritas, integritas, veritas* [Clarity, integrity, truth] . . .

In Arizona, weather is indeed Truth. To witness it selectively — to hibernate all summer in a refrigerated cave or shun the high country when blizzards pose threats to travel plans — is to miss much of what the land has to offer.

I willingly go out when the weather promises its worst, because that is often when the landscape delivers its best.

Based on that experience, I attribute *eight* seasons to the year, twice the standard allotment.

Arizona's climate is too extravagant and too moody to stuff into the convenient niches of spring, summer, fall, and winter. Spring appears in different makeup from time to time, erupting in the desert with ephemeral waterfalls one year and wildflowers the next. Summer splits into two distinct seasons, hot and dry and hot and wet; and on the cusp between them comes a mini-season of forest and grassland fire. Floods, not at all rare in arid Arizona, readily visit in summer or winter and constitute an unpredictably appearing season all their own. It almost sounds like a parade of Biblical plagues, except that the fury of all these events comes wrapped within a profound natural beauty.

Just be careful out there. In 1997, a flash flood swept 11 hikers to their deaths in Antelope Canyon, a deep, narrow sandstone slot near the Arizona-Utah border. In Tucson's Sabino Canyon, a young woman was carrying her baby on a peaceful afternoon walk when a thunderstorm rumbled over the ridge, surely a dramatic and mesmerizing sight, and killed them both with a single lightning bolt. The beauty and malignancy of the climate are eternal mates. There is no way to divorce them. ⊠

Edward Abbey wrote, "Each stone, each plant, each grain of sand exists in and for itself with a clarity that is undimmed by any suggestion of a different realm:" Just south of Arizona's border with Mexico, the Gran Desierto (above) looms as a stark environment softened by plants such as the desert lily (foreground), birdcage evening primrose, and sand verbena.

Be careful out there. Eight hikers were swept to their deaths by a flash flood in Antelope Canyon, a deep, narrow sandstone slot near the Arizona-Utah border: Ancient sand grains (right) were molded into sandstone before being carved into the swirling patterns in Antelope Canyon.

*The beauty and malignancy of the climate
are eternal mates:* A thunderstorm partially
veils the Sierra Estrella Mountains
southwest of Phoenix.

Water Music

I never feel entirely well except when I am among scenes of unspoiled nature.

— Ludwig van Beethoven, 1826

IT IS MARCH 1993, AND ALL ARIZONA is whining about the weather. We have endured weeks of dark, rainy skies, slick roads, and soggy fairways. The Pacific winter storm express has jumped its track, and Seattle's winter has pulled into our station instead.

Phil Norton, my trail companion, and I have come to a place where we will hear no complaints. We can hardly even hear each other speak — but no matter; the setting makes talk too cheap to matter. We are in Ventana Canyon, 1,100 feet above Tucson in the Santa Catalina Mountains. The entire canyon carries the din of water slamming on gneiss and granite — rivulets becoming creeks, whitewater corkscrewing over rocks, waterfalls blurting over surprise escarpments. The Catalinas are masquerading as the Cascades.

Hiking in these conditions challenges us. Eight times we've had to surge through water almost up to our hips as we work our way up Ventana Creek, normally a maze of dry boulders snoozing in the sun. Finally Phil and I pick our way off trail — with care — and find a ledge where we can sit and watch the action.

From this aerie we can see, and hear, three waterfalls converging from different directions and crashing into a pool 50 feet below. Phil finds a word to describe the moment, and it comes to him in Spanish: *Encantamiento.* Enchantment. I focus on the splashing counterpoint, the baroque trio sonata of three liquid instruments, each with its own distinct voice and melody, and think of an orchestral suite Handel composed for a riverboat party almost three centuries ago: *Water Music.*

Encountering water in any form in an arid land should delight us. And Arizonans certainly love water as long as it doesn't arrive inconveniently, aborting a golf date or flooding a family room. We have invented our own water spectacles, from 266-square-mile Lake Powell to the 560-foot-high geyser in Fountain Hills. We have been so enthused about water that, in 1987, the Arizona Legislature, finally worried about plunging water tables, banned developers from filling any more ornamental lakes with precious groundwater.

But water's most enchanting appearances in Arizona have always been Nature's own. They are evanescent, changing and disappearing with the seasons, and usually modest in scale. They come in the form of little creeks, seasonal waterfalls, and *tinajas* — a Spanish word that means, essentially, water holes in the rocks.

Water makes music here wherever it appears; it opens up whole new dimensions in Nature. Stare at the reflections of red rock and sky in Sedona's Seven Sacred Pools, and you will begin to understand why someone had thought to term them "sacred:" They celebrate and weave together water and light, two of the essentials of all life. Ephemeral waterfalls, thin as rice noodles, tumble off near-vertical cliffs in Oak Creek Canyon whenever the snow melts. Tiny streams meander down through the canyons and foothills of the

Water's most enchanting appearances have always been Nature's own: Seven Falls (right) flows year-round in the Santa Catalina Mountains north of Tucson.

Catalinas, sparkling like veins of silver in the bright desert sun — water in a far more affable mood than the chocolate mud that rages through the arroyos during a monsoon.

A century or two back, water music in these deserts was no rarity. The aquifers lay close to the surface, then, and they would bubble up as springs that nourished grassy *cienagas*, or marshes, and woods of mesquite, cottonwood, and willow trees. These underground rivers helped sustain the modest agriculture of the indigenous peoples, the

Weaving together water and light, a celebration of the essentials of all life: Turning leaves crystallize the sunlight (left) on the banks of Oak Creek in red rock country. Nearing West Fork, the creek stills briefly in a pool (above) sequined with leaves and fringed with grasses.

Hohokam and then the Pimas, for nearly 2,000 years. As recently as 1880, the Santa Cruz River rippled year round through Tucson as did the Salt River through Phoenix. Now, canals, dams, irrigation systems, and the straws of some 4 million urban Arizonans have sucked the rivers dry. The tradeoff is, well, the existence of urban Arizona.

Essayist Bruce Berger, who used to live in Phoenix, once wrote an appreciation of the city's hundreds of miles of canals. In less complicated times, he recalled, the water ditches served as Phoenix's social and recreational centers.

"Water skiing at 50 miles per hour in a canal 50 feet wide took skill . . . people accepted the dangers in the same way they tolerated swimming with dead cats, dogs, and snakes."

But Berger also mused about what Phoenix and the Salt River Valley might have been today if "enough water had been left [in the Salt River] to maintain riverbanks of cottonwood and willow, with habitat for tanagers, otters, and herons . . ."

Tempe's ambitious effort to revive the Salt River, filling the dead channel with the recently completed Tempe Town Lake, adds a new watery gleam to the desert floor — but for only two miles of the river's course through the valley.

Through the replumbing of Arizona, we have gained striking benefits: vast citrus groves and cotton fields, usually effective flood control, recreational lakes no desert ever imagined on its own, and parks and lawns moist and green enough to make the arid land lose its strangeness for the newcomers thronging here. In return, much of the water music has been silenced.

But the music still plays out there, abundant enough for anyone willing to take the trouble to find it and listen. It adds the grace notes that embellish the desert — with nothing less than life itself. ⌧

Water opens up new dimensions in Nature: Cienega Creek (left) in the Empire/Cienega Conservation Area southeast of Tucson nourishes a wetlands in the midst of a desert.

Dams have stopped the flow of the Salt River at Phoenix: Upstream, at Horseshoe Bend (above), the river slices through the Sonoran Desert's stands of saguaro cactus.

Tiny streams meander through canyons and foothills: Pine Creek
(left) threads over a staircase of mossy rocks and ferns. West Clear
Creek (right) slides over a hanging garden into a forest wilderness
on the Mogollon Rim.

DAVID MUENCH

We have invented our own water spectacles: Lake Powell (above), with a shoreline of about 2,000 miles, provides fishing, boating, and other recreation for tens of thousands of people in what once was a seldom visited, starkly beautiful Glen Canyon. The Petrified Forest National Park (right) protects Lithodendron Wash in the Painted Desert.

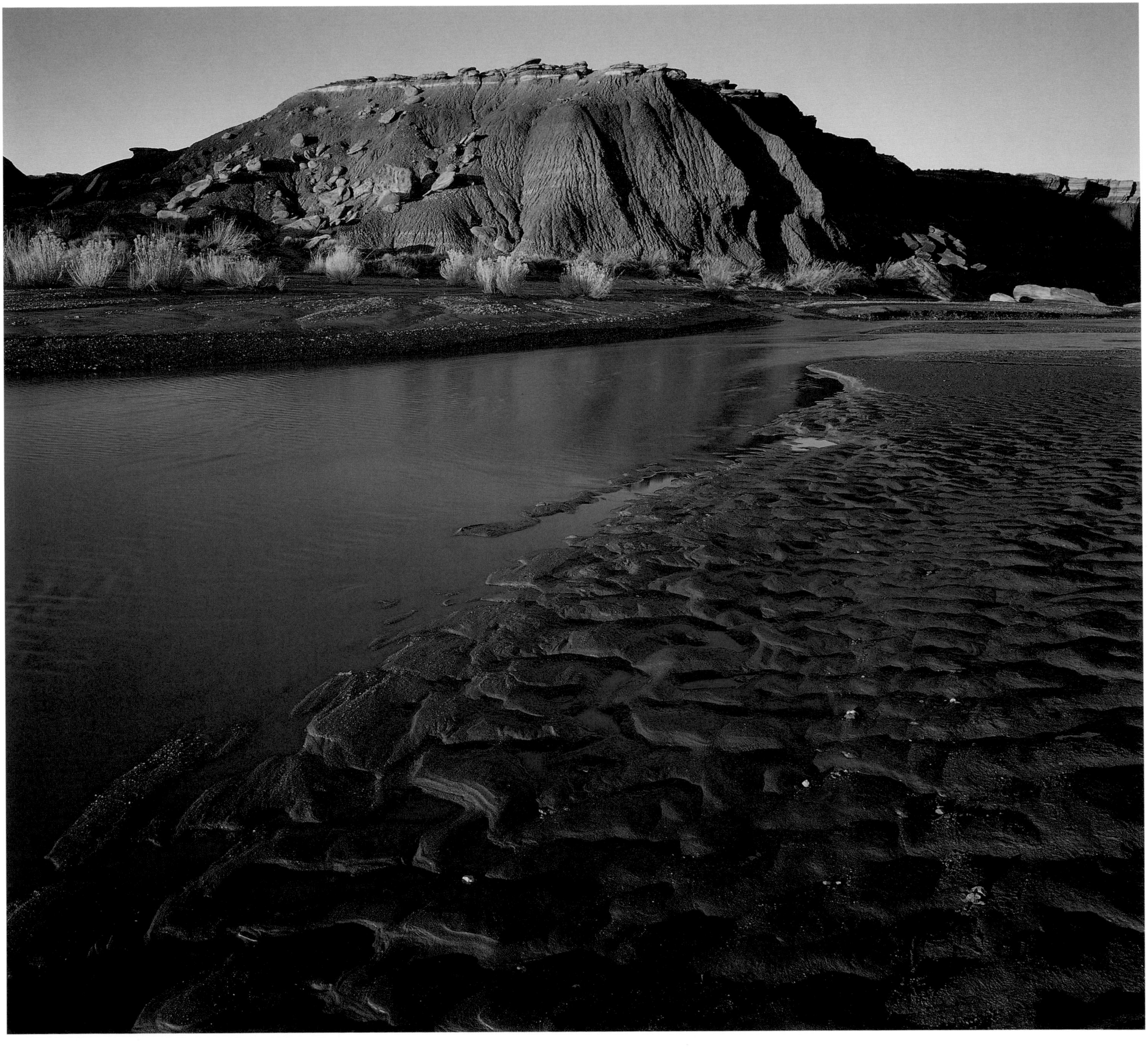

JACK DYKINGA

Water music still plays out there for anyone willing to take the trouble to find it and listen: The Salt River (above), essentially a desert stream, originates in the White Mountains with the confluence of the White and Black rivers. Swollen by runoff (right), the river charges over its rocky course.

Water embellishes the desert: Ribbon Falls (left) and Elves Chasm (above) lie deep inside the Grand Canyon, which from its rims appears to be a dry, rocky desert riddled with canyons and ridges.

Evanescent, changing and disappearing with the seasons: A spring waterfall (above) splashes into a pool in the Santa Catalina Mountains. Josephine Wash (right), in the Santa Rita Mountains south of Tucson, greens up during an August runoff.

Betting on the Blooms

*Aside from the blossoms upon bush and tree there are few bright petals
shining in the desert. It is no place for flowers.*

— John C. Van Dyke, *The Desert,* 1901

NEARLY EVERYONE WHO WRITES about the Southwestern deserts today rightly pays tribute to Van Dyke, but on this matter of bright petals, he was dead wrong. Arizona, against all odds, is a splendid place for flowers. The unlucky professor simply dropped by in the wrong years when he roamed the desert a century ago.

His unfortunate timing isn't surprising. There are many more wrong years than right ones, at least as far as we spectacle-obsessed humans are concerned. But Nature, concerned with survival, doles out a parsimonious frequency. The great desert wildflower explosions, which occur maybe every three or five or 10 years — the intervals are as unpredictable as dice — appear as often as needed to service the web of life, and no more.

If there were a textbook formula for triggering a good spring wildflower crop, it would include a fall and winter of steady rain, meaning at least an inch each month from October through March. But the flowers are too capricious to follow a formula. Such a rain quota may arrive in perfect compliance, and spring still will dawn with a bonanza of sweet green grasses and seedlings, but few blooms.

No scientific formula exists for reliably predicting the flowers. Nobody yet knows the full ecological story.

Mark Dimmitt, director of natural history at the Arizona-Sonora Desert Museum in Tucson, admits: "Predicting a good bloom is nearly impossible until it's about to begin."

Dimmitt at least has some well-educated guesses about the bloom-and-bust cycle. It's triggered by a soggy El Niño winter, such as the one in 1997-98. Next comes an unusually lavish blooming season, with carpets of Sonoran Desert poppies, penstemons, marigolds, fairy dusters, and hundreds of other flowering species. Such a spike in the food source ripples up through the food chain, so there will be as much as 30 times the normal population of mice and ground squirrels tearing though this buffet. Whatever the following winter's weather, Dimmitt says, the ravenous rodents almost

Rare as they are, the flowers play a vital role in the web of life on this seemingly harsh land: A hummingbird (above) feeds on flower nectar and spreads the pollen. Mexican poppies (the yellow flowers at right) and lupine share a field in the Superstition Mountains east of Phoenix.

surely have eaten into the seed bank for the next wildflower bloom.

But no studies yet have pinned down this cycle.

Rare as they are, the flowers play a vital role in the web of life on this seemingly harsh land. When the flowers appear, their nectar nourishes their pollinators — bats, hummingbirds, butterflies, and bees — by the billions. (A thousand species of bees live in the Sonoran Desert.) When the annuals fail to bloom, their dormant seeds sustain the rodents and quail in lean years. (Scientists have found as many as 200,000 seeds buried in one square meter of Sonoran Desert.) In good years, these small animals become food for predators such as coyotes, bobcats, and raptors; in bad years the casualties of starva-

tion become fodder for the scavengers, the vultures and ravens, flies and ants. Nature's big picture, as always, is perfectly composed and balanced.

Some locations produce better wildflower shows than others. The skirts of Picacho Peak, an eroded remnant of tilted layers of lava flows, are famous for spring riots of Mexican gold poppies and lavender spikes of lupine. In the Mojave Desert, dandelions, desert primrose, and woolly marigolds burst from banks of desiccated washes. Nobody knows why, but the fertility may have something to do with ancient soils that still haven't eroded.

Defying common sense, drier places offer more lavish flower displays than wet ones. The reason is that the most dramatic flow-

A spike in the food source ripples up through the food chain: Mice and ground squirrels feast on buffets such as this brittlebush-studded hillside (left) in Organ Pipe Cactus National Monument. As the rodent populations swell, so does that of coyotes (above), which search the fields for rodents.

ers are annuals, blooming just once before dying. On parched lands, longer-lived perennials such as mesquite and creosote are fewer and farther between, so they offer less competition for water and sunlight when the opportunistic annuals appear.

High Southwestern elevations likewise can deliver spectacular flower displays, but on a different schedule. Prime time for wildflowers in the Southwest's alpine forests is the monsoon season, July into September — and the volume can be incredible. When Gen. George Crook led his U.S. Army troops across the Mogollon Plateau in the summer of

1871, they tramped across "a carpet of colors which would rival the best examples of the looms of Turkey or Persia," wrote the expedition's journalist, Capt. John G. Bourke.

The variety, too, is astounding. Golden columbine, a flower that trails a spray of curled yellow tentacles, could be cast close-up in a science-fiction movie. The rubber rabbit-brush, whose humble yellow flowers appear in the fall so they don't have to compete with the beauty queens of summer for pollinators, looks like blooms on the moon amid the black crater-pocked plateau east of Flagstaff.

This spectacle of seemingly delicate wild-

flowers dressing up a harsh, combative landscape poses a perplexing contrast, like a burly lumberjack wearing a cashmere vest to work. Sometimes the struggle of opposite moods occurs on the same plant, as in the barrel cactus's ravishing blooms rising out of a platoon of clawlike bayonets.

It's tempting to suppose that Nature offers her amends with these bouquets, an occasional gift to make up for her vicious rampages of torrential floods, stifling heat, and murderous droughts. Nothing could be further from the truth. Her extravagance is simply part of her sense of balance. ⌗

High Southwestern elevations can deliver spectacular flower displays, too: Locoweed (left), princely daisy, Fendler's sandwort, and Colorado rubberweed flowers sprout amidst native grasses in the Apache National Forest in northern Arizona. Golden columbine (above) and monkeyflowers bloom in the late summer in the Galiuro Mountains in the southeastern part of the state.

DAVID MUENCH ▷

Arizona, against all odds, is a splendid place for flowers: A Sonoran Desert hillside (left) riots with the carnival colors of Mexican gold poppies and lupine. Preserved as the home of its namesake, Organ Pipe Cactus National Monument (right) also nourishes flowers in its craggy terrain.

Defying common sense, drier places offer more lavish flower displays than wet ones: In the Mohawk Dunes (above), primroses form a ring in a clump of purple sand verbena. Fiddleneck and owl clover (right) don't mind the dryness of Organ Pipe Cactus National Monument.

Prime time for wildflowers in the Southwest's alpine forests is the monsoon season, July into September: Locoweed (above) fills a meadow in the White Mountains, and cutleaf coneflower (right) blooms at Hannagan Meadow in the Apache National Forest.

GARY LADD ▷

This spectacle of seemingly delicate wildflowers dressing up a harsh, combative landscape poses a perplexing contrast: In the Flagstaff area's Bonito Park (left), prairie sunflowers mix with native grasses below Sunset Crater Volcano. Farther north (above), in what sometimes is called slickrock country, mules ears sunflowers stand out in sharp contrast to the distant sandstone formations of the Paria Canyon-Vermilion Cliffs Wilderness.

Dry Bones

*The hand of the Lord was upon me, and carried me out in the spirit of the Lord,
and set me down in the midst of the valley which was full of bones.*

— Ezekiel 37:1

JACK DYKINGA

JUNE, THE DRIEST MONTH, CON-
jures the season of bones. Deer tibia, sheep
ribs, coyote skulls, articulated rattler cartilage.
Woody skeletons of cholla and saguaro cac-
tuses, which stand determinedly for up to 30
years after their demise. The bones of animal
and plant litter the desert valleys, jut from arroyo banks, gape passively back at the relent-
less sun as it tries, impossibly, to bleach more
life out of them. It recalls the Old Testament,
another desert book, bristling with hostility
and tragedy.

But Georgia O'Keeffe taught us a new way
to look at bones — as art, as an essential part
of the architecture of life, as more of the
many components of the desert's natural
beauty. After O'Keeffe, desert bones could be
high art or low kitsch, paintings worth a million dollars or lamp bases for sale in curio
shops. Author Charles Bowden, one of the
Sonoran Desert's most articulate apostles,
suggests that the desert is the one place where
we need not fear dying: "Here death is like
breathing. Here death simply is."

We say "bone dry," which describes this land in June. We call a color "bone white," and that is almost the midday sky in summer's first phase — the pigment leached out of it, the light "fierce and hot as a rain of meteors," as Van Dyke saw it. The apparent stillness, the shortage of color, the improbability of rain (one-fifth of an inch in an average Phoenix June), the bones across the landscape — it all feels like some ancient, abandoned land, a primeval place where finality is the prime attraction.

First looks, as usual, deceive. Even in the desert, summer's opening act teems with activity, a testament to the earth's determination to meet its obligations no matter what extreme measures are required.

Look closely at the mesquite, whose stingy, ant-sized leaves fold up during summer days to conserve moisture. At the same time, its plump lime-green seed pods swell luxuriantly. Two centuries ago, native people pounded and ground these pods into protein-rich flour. Packrats still bank them. Bees, beetles, weevils, assassin bugs, and tarantula-hawk wasps thrive in the mesquite's umbrella. If you want to visit a baby saguaro cactus, check under a mesquite. The filigreed shade literally nurses the cactus through its first critical decades of life, protecting it from the intense sun. Through the 1960s, '70s, and '80s, the mature saguaro population began decreasing in Saguaro National Park, and alarm bells clamored. Suspects included a bacterial epidemic and urban air pollution. It turned out that miners and soldiers in the late 1800s had stripped this same land of mesquite and paloverde trees for wood to feed their kilns and stoves, depriving young saguaros of their nurses. When century-old saguaros began dying of old age in the 1960s, a whole middle-aged generation behind them was missing in action.

As human senses adjust to the minimalism of the desert summer, its commotion becomes apparent. Many animals are hibernating in burrows during the long day, but some have adapted to the heat more

It feels like a primeval place where finality is the prime attraction: A javelina skull (left) lies in a patch of teddy bear cholla. A turkey vulture (top right) can ease its survival workload by gliding with thermals. A zebra-tail lizard (right) hugs a rock to cool itself.

actively. Harris hawks and turkey vultures glide on the thermals, hitching a free ride on the hot rising air. Gambel's quail peck nervously at the sun-baked ground, but they have much more to fear from the hawks than the heat; they can endure losing half their body weight from dehydration. (Lose a mere tenth of body weight, and a human is in trouble.) Zebra-tail lizards sprint across the scorched ground like striped darts; although their skinny bodies heat up rapidly in the sun, they cool down just as quickly by hugging a shaded rock. Jackrabbits survive the summer — unless those hawks get them — by pumping their blood through radiators of tiny veins in their enormous ears. Incidentally, radiating jackrabbits face north in hot weather, exposing their ears to the coolest horizon. As biologists keep learning, Nature's logic is on best display under the worst conditions.

Nature's art gallery may seem meager in these conditions; photographers whine about work days squeezed into half hours just before sunrise and after sunset. True enough.

First looks, as usual, deceive: Monument Valley (right) hardly seems a place where animals can survive, but look at the trail (right, foreground) left by a pack rat (left, bottom). A Harris hawk (left, middle) makes a home amidst the sharp spines of a saguaro cactus. Such a raptor poses more of a threat to Gambel's quail (left, top) than does summer's heat and dryness.

But aridity, like every other facet of Nature, creates its own fashions.

Dunes, for example, are sculpted when wind blows dry grains of sand into a crest, which grows until gravity demands an avalanche. Connoisseurs compare them to ocean waves — from Monument Valley's ankle-high ripples to 600-foot tsunamis of sand in the Gran Desierto in Mexico, just south of the Arizona-Sonora border. Dry, cracked clay, the consequence of a hot sun sucking the moisture out of a puddle, may seem like the very essence of desolation, but look again: Its geometry radiates the intricacy of a spider's web. And the air — seldom violated by a single cloud in June, it suspends enough dust to form monochromatic sunsets so intensely yellow or orange or red that they color not only the sky but also the entire landscape. The show may evaporate in a minute, but like the waterfalls and wildflowers of a wetter season, these sunsets become all the more precious for their brief display.

Loren Eiseley, a wise naturalist and anthropologist, once wrote a modest essay immodestly titled *The Secret of Life*, in which he advocated prowling the outdoors in late autumn, after the leaves had fallen and the birds had scrambled south. "There is an unparalleled opportunity," he wrote, "to examine in sharp and beautiful angularity the shape of life without its disturbing muddle of juices and leaves."

Eiseley spent most of his life on the Great Plains. But like Ezekiel, he would have appreciated Arizona's severity and clarity in June. The season of bones, the time of revelations. ▨

Aridity creates its own fashions: When dust floats in the atmosphere (left), a rising or setting sun colors an entire landscape, including this cholla cactus skeleton. A skeletal cholla branch (above) rests among Mexican gold poppies.

Dunes are sculpted when wind blows dry grains of sand into a crest: The Gran Desierto
(left) in Mexico accounts for a portion of the Sonoran Desert.

Woody skeletons stand determinedly for up to 30 years after their demise: A saguaro skeleton
(above) maintains its place with its comrades on a ridge in the Tucson Mountains.

Georgia O'Keeffe taught us to look at bones and other desert elements as art: The white of a desert bighorn sheep's jawbone (right) frames a bunch of purple mat flowers. Sand verbena (above) spread out on the textured ripples of a sand dune.

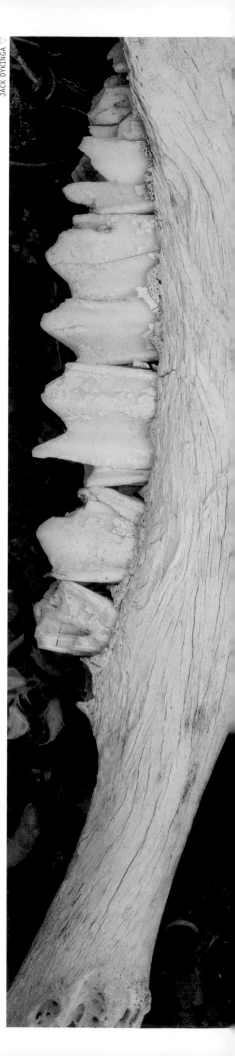

On the desert, death simply is: Arching saguaro ribs (left) gracefully
frame columns of organ pipe cactus and silvery brittlebush in flower.
Mexican gold poppies (above) bloom against a downed saguaro.

The bones of animals litter the desert: The sun has bleached all color from mule deer antlers (right) surrounded by Mexican gold poppies.

Natural elements spread a geometry as intricate as a spider's web: Saguaro cactus ribs (left) sprawl over a field of owl clover, and a chunk of petrified wood (above) rests on a bed of Chinle Formation mudstone cracked by water, sun, and wind.

Rhythms of Fire

Nature, as we know her, is no saint.

— Ralph Waldo Emerson, "Experience"

ALL AROUND, IT WAS THE HOTTEST week in Arizona since anyone began keeping records, so hot that on June 26, 1990, Phoenix Sky Harbor Airport shut down because many jetliners lack operating specifications for temperatures above 120° F. On that afternoon, thermometers hit 122° in Phoenix, 110° in Sedona, and 106° even in Payson, up in the normally cool pines.

But there wasn't anything "normal" about the Mogollon Rim forests that week. Spring had been unusually dry, and in concert with the hellish summer heat, the pines were parched. Scientists measuring the moisture content of logs on the forest floor found them as dry as kiln-dried lumber. Living trees were not much better off.

And in the long view of Nature, these forests hadn't been "normal" for much of this century, not since modern humans began tampering with the natural rhythms of fire. Left to take care of itself, a southwestern piñon-juniper woodland would have a fire every 20 to 30 years; and a blaze would sweep through a taller ponderosa forest every two to 10 years. These are considered "good" fires, cleansing fires. They consume the brush and dead pine needle thatch and thin out the smaller, weaker trees. But ever since Smokey the Bear was a cub, we have fought forest fires with vigorous public relation campaigns and steadily improving technology, so by the summer of 1990, the forest between Payson and the Mogollon Rim was like a vast firepit stuffed with kindling.

Early on the afternoon of June 25, a dry, wheezing thunderstorm coalesced over the rim — the 2,000-foot-high escarpment frequently builds its own weather — and a lightning bolt crackled into a tree in the foothills of the rocky wall. The temperature was 105° F. Within two hours the fire had blossomed to more than 100 acres, and — ominously — it started to scramble up the rim.

Tim Grier, a Forest Service fire information officer, was working Forest Road 300 that afternoon, videotaping the fire from the scenic lip of the rim. His video shows the sky

A dry spring and hellishly hot summer parch the pine forests: A smoke column rises (left) from the Bearjaw Fire in the San Francisco Peaks area north of Flagstaff. A firefighter (right) douses flames on a pine.

turning unearthly shades of amber, orange, pink, red-brown, blood-red. Flames glimmer meekly through the smoke, then suddenly explode, rearing into the sky like crimson stallions, assaulting whole football fields of forest in one leap. Now the *fire* is making its own weather, furious convection currents that ferry embers up to spawn new blazes on top of the rim.

"Most of the time when someone talks about '300-foot flames' in a forest fire, there's not a lot of truth in it," Grier recalls, sober with the memory. "There was that day."

The Dude Fire, named for the creek near its origin, quickly took a tragic turn. It killed six firefighters who were ambushed when another dry thunderstorm expelled a burst of wind straight down.

"Usually, we describe a fire as having a head and a tail," Grier says. "For half an hour, this fire had four heads. It spread in every direction."

In the seven days until the Dude Fire was

contained, it burned 45 square miles, chased nearly 1,200 people out of their homes, and destroyed 75 houses and cabins, including Zane Grey's own historic home.

Ten years later, the Tonto National Forest offers an instructive and eerily scenic self-guided auto tour of the burn area below the Mogollon Rim northeast of Payson. Ash-gray snags of ponderosa, piñon, and juniper stretch into a sapphire sky, abstract sculptures and organic tombstones silently commemorating a war. Meanwhile, evergreen seedlings and wildflowers riot at their feet. It's impossible not to feel a sense of joy at the explosion of rebirth and renewal. But the renewal required human intervention.

The fire destroyed the vegetation locking down the topsoil, and the heavy summer rains that followed began to wash it away. Hurriedly, the Forest Service reseeded the burn area to slow erosion and provide forage for wildlife. Still, it will be about a century before the ponderosa forest returns to its mature splendor.

In the short term, the Dude Fire fanned new public interest in what foresters call fire ecology. More of us are beginning to understand what the Forest Service and Park Service had concluded — even as they had Smokey rag us to put out those campfires — that natural, lightning-sparked forest fires are a normal and essential part of Nature's housekeeping. Periodic small fires help prevent the big catastrophic ones and keep the mature forest healthy and productive. In selected cases, forest managers now let lightning fires burn, and they set fires — "controlled burns" — to clear out kindling-like brush from too-dense growth.

But treating Nature right stumbles increasingly over social reality here in the 21st century, as more and more of us retire to cabins in the woods, and mushrooming suburbs ooze onto once-wild land.

The 1995 Rio Fire in north Scottsdale, which threatened hundreds of expensive new homes trickling into the lush desert foothills of the McDowell Mountains, had to be ex-

tinguished — there was no legitimate alternative. Fire ecologists called it an "urban/wildland interface fire," a relatively new phenomenon. Where pioneers once cleared wide swaths of land around their homesteads that served as firebreaks, today's tree- and cactus-hugging ex-urbanites crave snuggling up to the natural environment around them as intimately as possible. When Nature decides it's time for a fire, unnatural measures have to be taken to stop her. In the long run, these disrupt her ritual rhythms — rain, drought, fire, rebirth. And invite her revenge, eventually. ⊠

Fire consumes the brush and dead pine needle thatch and thins out the smaller, weaker trees: Flames (left) from a dry forest floor pounce on trees. Firefighters (above) smother ground flames.

It's impossible not to feel a sense of joy at the explosion of rebirth and renewal: New growth (left and right) reclaims an area burned three years previously.

Periodic small fires help prevent the big catastrophic ones and keep the mature forest healthy: Looking like charred toothpicks, this sweeping expanse of burned forest (above) is but a sliver of the Dude Fire's damage as seen from the Mogollon Rim. Snags — the standing remains of trees — are reminders of a fire in the Chiricahua Mountains (right) in southeastern Arizona.

Seedlings and wildflowers riot at the feet of burned trees: Goosefoot (left) and fleabane (above) are a part of the recovery process.

It will be about a century before forests like these return to mature splendor: Mount Elden (above), near Flagstaff, seems to be a tombstone for a dead area. An eerie beauty arises on a Mount Graham burn area (right) in southeastern Arizona.

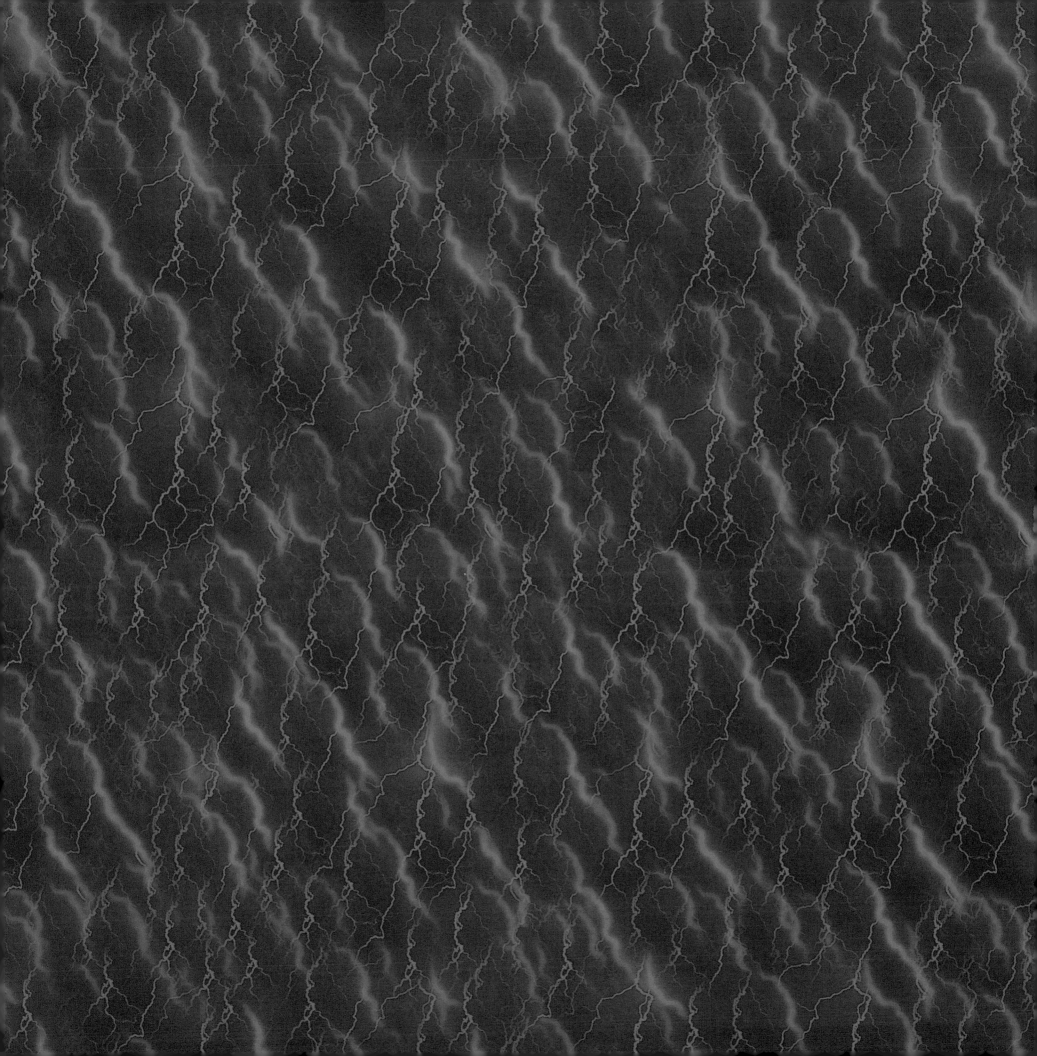

Bruised Skies

With the far darkness made of the he-rain on the ends of your wings, come to us soaring.

— Navajo Night Chant

▽ GEORGE STOCKING

MORNING DAWNS WITH SEARING clarity and brilliance and with the too-familiar promise of convection-oven midday heat that has dominated the last 30 or 45 or even 60 days. Even the most stoic among us are cursing the Season of Bones. After so many days, the heat is a vise tightening on the psyche. There's an urgency every morning to get things done — walk the dog, sweep the sidewalk, tee off for nine quick holes — before retreating to air-conditioned hibernation by midmorning. Venture out later, and the heat and light press palpably against the body. You feel yourself becoming small and leathery, a hardening raisin.

But this is the beginning of July, and something seems vaguely different. A slight tension hovers in the morning air, an intimation of two elements uneasily beginning to mingle. The interloper is a whiff of hu-

midity, ever so slight, announcing its annual challenge to the desert aridity. If you've lived here long enough, you recognize the subtle signals, and you organize the rest of the day so as to be near a window, a porch, some form of lookout.

Around noon, tentative cotton puffs materialize in the sky, crowning a mountain range or conferring over the southern horizon. Over the next couple of hours, they begin to build, piling up like puffy dumplings being stacked by an invisible chef. If you're lucky, they begin to move in your direction. Invisible ions flirt and dance, the white masses darken and churn and shove, ugly threats begin to rumble. If this were Kansas, it'd be time to call in Toto and check out the basement.

The sun slips behind the storm front, its first blink since Easter. The rumbling grows angrier and more insistent as the leading

edges of the dumplings take the shapes of giant fists and knuckles. The sky becomes the spectrum of a bad bruise — charcoal, purple, olive. An ancient odor, languid with humidity, burdens the air. *Crrrakkk!* — the first pitchfork of lightning burns into a ridge a few miles away. The violence, slow but dramatic in the preliminaries, has spilled over whatever meteorological dam was holding it back. Any right-thinking human or coyote is under cover at this point.

The rain begins as drops so plump they thud into the desiccated earth like beanbags, launching geysers of dust when they land. The bombardment accelerates, the drops clustering into a shower, then into sheets, then a wall of hammering water. More lightning stings the sky. The burnt aroma of ozone permeates the air. The temperature dives, 20 degrees in 10 minutes. Out of nowhere a gale

The interloper is a whiff of humidity, announcing its annual challenge to the desert aridity: Clouds linger (above) over the Superstition Mountains east of the Phoenix metropolitan area. A storm (right) sends columns of rain onto the desert outside Tucson.

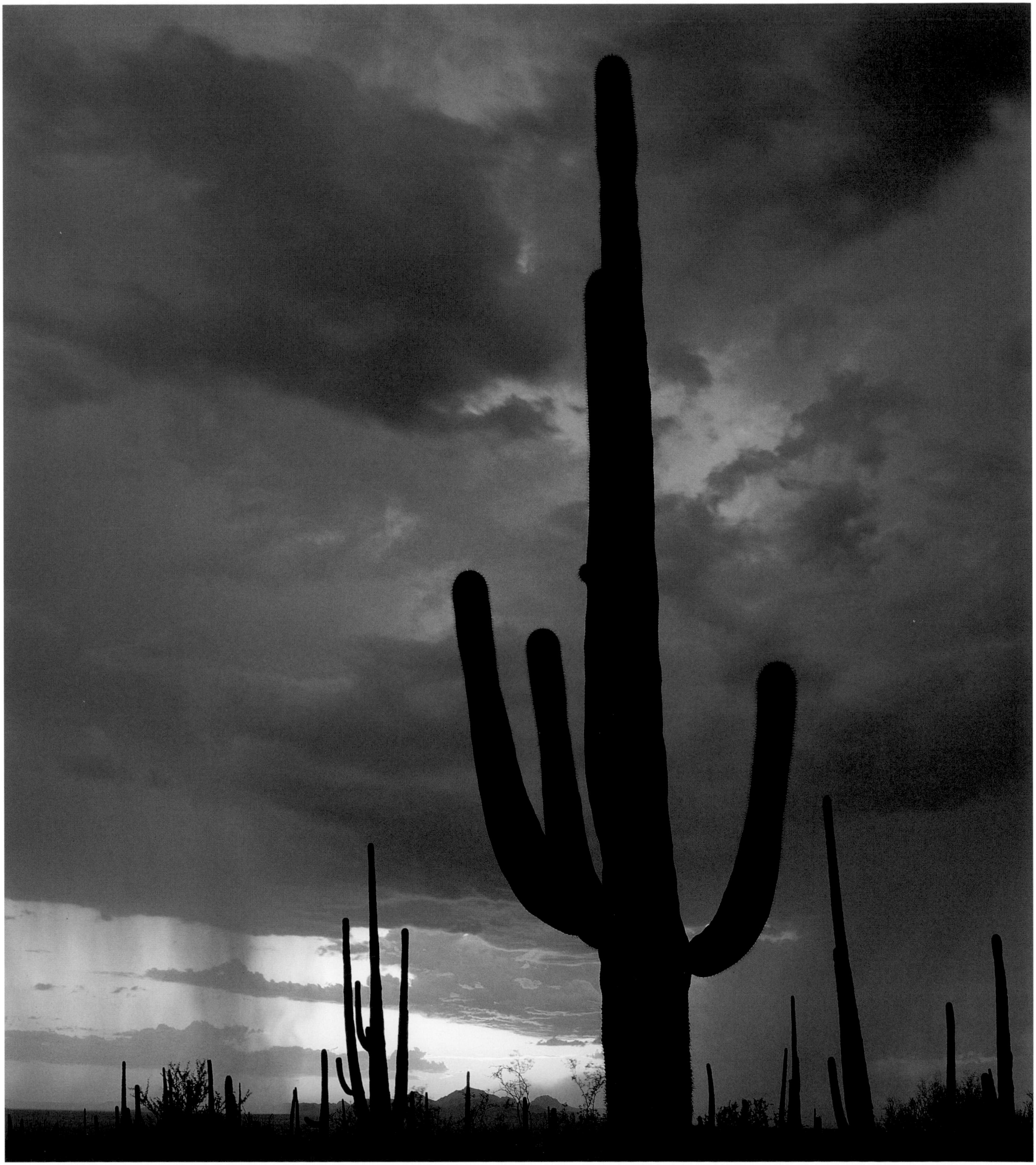

JACK DYKINGA

joins the frenzy, whipping the deluge into a frontal assault. Its ferocity is incredible; an inch of rain in half an hour isn't uncommon. (On one July day in 1958, Tucson recorded 3.98 inches of rain — a third of its annual norm.)

And then, as quickly as it came, the storm diminishes, fading to a light sprinkle. The thunder throttles back to a surly grumble. The sky's malignant greens and purples begin to shift to less threatening parts of the spectrum — mousy grays and shadowy blues. A rip appears in the cloud cover, and a slash of late afternoon sunlight breaks through, burnishing a hill or a clump of buildings with coppery light. Earth and atmosphere metabolize the moisture so quickly that an hour later, it won't even be muddy. A few casualties testify to the storm's passage — downed branches, a tall saguaro or an unlucky urban palm tree fried by a lightning strike. Left over is an odd coolness in the air and the sweet pungent perfume of wet creosote bush, which smells like camphor, pine, and the

imagined memory of ancient evenings on the desert, long before the advent of civilization.

We call this the monsoon, not incorrectly. Originally the word arose from the Arabic *mawsim*, or season. According to the World Meterological Organization, "monsoon" now may be used to describe any continental-scaled seasonal change brought on by a shift in the prevailing winds. Some years back, there was a movement to substitute the Spanish word *chubasco*, "downpour," but it failed to click with our vocabularies. The Navajo recognize rain in two genders, this summer "he-rain" being the moody, violent one. The Tohono O'odham, or "desert people," call the monsoon *Jukiabig Mashath*, "moon of the rains."

Actually, it's usually two moons of the rains — along with thunder, lightning, wind, hail, floods, and, on very rare occasions, funnel clouds. The monsoon traditionally begins around the end of the first week of July and dribbles away in early September, although the actual dates in a given year can drift a week or two either way. Science tells

The sky becomes the spectrum of a bad bruise: A storm (right) focuses on the western part of Phoenix

us exactly when the monsoon is in season: an average daily dew point of at least 55° F (the dew point is the temperature at which moisture can condense in the air, which we feel as mugginess).

The Southwest's gentler winter rains come courtesy of the Pacific Ocean. The westerly storm track carries moisture inland, where the cold masses of desert mountain ranges reach up and condense it as rain (or snow). In the spring, the storm track shifts toward the north, and the Southwest dries out and heats up. The increasing heat creates a pocket of low pressure that eventually draws the damp summer breath of the Sea of Cortez and the Gulf of Mexico. When the Mexican moisture finally streams into the Southwest, rising convection currents can build spectacular cumulonimbus architecture as high as 40,000 feet. There is a vast amount of water and energy in these towering cloud masses, which is why the monsoon is so visually extravagant.

And monsoons pack a wide repertoire of mischief. Monsoon storms regularly wash out roads and hiking trails, trigger rockslides, ignite fires, kill saguaros, and knock out electrical power systems. Wise Southwesterners shut off computers whenever he-rain comes stomping around. Dust storms whipped by dry monsoons are a serious highway hazard; a July storm in 1995 caused a 21-car pileup on Interstate 10 between Phoenix and Tucson. On the plus side of the ledger, a good storm scrubs urban air clean of visible pollution, and up north in the red rocks and canyon country, it intensifies every color in an already flamboyant landscape.

For the thirsty land, the monsoon season is a blessing. The ponderosa forests, dry as straw in June, absorb some fire insurance. Bears ravage the berries triggered by the rain. Sacaton grasslands, common in the mile-high elevations of the Chihuahuan Desert, sleep through the spring and turn almost overnight from shredded-wheat pale to a healthy lime green. In the Sonoran Desert, the spidery ocotillo rouses from apparent death to sport fingernail-sized leaves, and the saguaro swells like a pregnant accordion, swilling as much as 200 gallons of water in a single rainstorm. Desert critters shift into action, not all of them welcome in civilized society, such as the palo verde root borer, a mouse-sized flying beetle that has terrorized house cats.

The storms form as small cells, sometimes less than a mile across, dump their payload in as little as five or 10 minutes, and dissipate. Sometimes, the lower atmosphere is so hot and dry that the downpour evaporates before it reaches the ground and hangs above the horizon like dark scratches against the sky. The Navajo call the dark scratches "the hair of clouds"; we use the word virga. Sometimes there's no payoff at all: The storm clouds clench charcoal fists, snarling and grumbling, then inexplicably lighten up and move on, like a bar fight that disperses before someone actually throws a punch. On any given square foot of Arizona, a threatened monsoon probably will fail two out of three times.

But the watery climax isn't a vital part of the show; the drama is there with or without it. The monsoon has inspired some of the Southwest's most evocative nature writing. Edward Abbey described the monsoon clouds as "anvil-headed giants with glints of lightning in their depths." Poet Richard Shelton saw them as "great white cathedrals." Back in 1895, when John Wesley Powell wrote the memoirs of his Grand Canyon expeditions, he characterized the clouds as fellow canyon explorers poking into gorges, "[seeming] to have wills and souls of their own, and to be going on diverse errands — a vast assemblage of self-willed clouds, faring here and there, intent upon purposes hidden in their own breasts."

The monsoon indeed seems to follow its own internal directive. Unpredictable, flirtatious, and always potentially dangerous, its annual visit reminds us that human civilization is not the ultimate force on the Southwestern landscape. The lesson in humility is good for our souls. So is the rain, usually. ⌧

A rip appears in the cloud cover, and a slash of late afternoon sunlight breaks through: A storm (left) hovers behind Buddha Temple in the Grand Canyon.

And then, as quickly as it comes, the storm diminishes: Lightning (left) strikes over Red Mountain east of Scottsdale. Seen from a Joshua tree forest (above), a storm slips away over a distant mountain.

*The Tohono O'odham, or "desert people," of southern Arizona call the
monsoon Jukiabig Mashath, "moon of the rains:"* Its fury spent (above), a
monsoon gently sprays the Quinlan Mountains area of the Tohono O'odham
Indian Reservation west of Tucson. Farther east (left), also at sunset, the
Avra Valley draws attention from a monsoon.

The Navajo recognize the summer "he-rain" as moody and violent:
Lightning (above) spreads slivers of electricity over Tucson.
This monsoon (right) trails distant wisps of virga, downpour that's
evaporating before it reaches the desert floor.

GEORGE STOCKING ▷

There is a vast amount of water and energy in these towering cloud masses, which is why the monsoon is so visually extravagant: Storms spread over broad areas, such as Jadito Wash (left) in northern Arizona and the Sierra Ancha Wilderness (above) in central Arizona.

Any right-thinking human or coyote is under cover at this point: A bruised sky spits lightning onto Monument Valley (above) and the Grand Canyon (right).

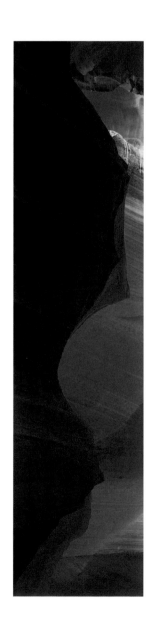

Water Furies

"This would be good country," a tourist says to me,
"if only you had some water."

— Edward Abbey, *Desert Solitaire,* 1968

IT IS A TYPICAL LATE SUMMER DAY IN the Grand Canyon, the midday mercury threatening 100° and the lingering monsoon pushing the humidity into the sultry zone — a fine day for a swim. Hikers are hanging out in Bright Angel Creek, their energetic kids building little rock dams to create swimming holes.

Around midafternoon, swarthy clouds begin to boil around the canyon rims a mile overhead. Lightning strafes the North Rim. Rain begins to patter. The swimmers wisely quit the creek. Nothing appears ominous to the tourists. But Sjors Horstman, who has worked and lived at Phantom Ranch for nine years, studying the canyon's beauty and treachery, knows enough to be concerned. He sweeps the creek to make certain everyone is out and well away from it.

"About 45 minutes later, I heard the roar," he later recalls. "I first thought it was thunder, but it kept going. Then I realized it was a flash flood."

The water comes crashing down Phantom Canyon, the first large side canyon north of the ranch and usually the first to "flash." The wave looks like liquid mud, the intense color of rich, red-brown chocolate, and it is 7 feet high. Freshly uprooted trees and chunks of irrigation pipe surf on its churning back. The wave dislodges boulders 6 feet in diameter and bounces them downstream like beachballs. Horstman feels the ground rumble with their passage. The creek rips away its own banks and devours brush and trees. Even the canyon air no longer smells like rain. It is muggy with mud.

The tantrum subsides quickly. In 10 minutes, the water level drops 2 feet. In another three hours, all is back to normal — except, Horstman says, "It was like a whole new creek bed. All the dams and swimming holes were gone, not a sign of them. Even my favorite rocks I always sat on were gone. Alongside the creek all the vegetation was ripped clean away. Above that, bushes were flattened. I found dead trout in them. As I watched, a great blue heron flew in to take advantage of the insects and fish exposed by the flood. Life goes on."

Indeed it does. Every so often, Nature pushes her own reset button and rearranges the furniture, quickly, dramatically, and without apology. Only humans see it as tragedy. In this flood, the witnesses were able to leave the canyon with nothing worse than a frightening memory. But just two days later — September 11, 1997 — the same creek went on a fresh rampage and swept two unwary hikers to their deaths. Their bodies were found two weeks later, 20 and 40 miles downriver — the Colorado River.

Southwestern children grow up with warnings constantly hammered in their ears: Don't cross a flooded wash. Stay out of canyon bottoms in monsoon season. Remember, it doesn't even have to be raining where you are for a flash flood to get you.

But this land is always flooded with newcomers and tourists, and many have never heard the warnings — or just can't believe them. Every year, people die. (And not only

The creek rips away its own banks and devours brush and trees: The dry bed of Aztec Creek (top) is grown in with grass until a flash flood (middle) tears through. The flood recedes quickly, revealing the aftermath (bottom) of torn vegetation and thick silt.

in the Southwest. Flash floods kill more Americans, an average of 160 annually, than any other natural hazard.)

Arizona's history is awash in stories of tragic floods, floods of Biblical fury — except that they often wreak their vengeance in 40 minutes, not 40 days.

On a cold, still-dark February morning in 1890, men at a prospector's camp on the Hassayampa River awoke to an infernal roar coming out of the black canyon above them. Torrential rains falling atop a deep snowpack had broken a cheaply built dam 15 miles upstream. Survivors described the front wave as a nearly perpendicular wall 50 feet high, eerily phosphorescent in the darkness. It killed about 50 people; the exact count was never established.

In the summer of 1947, a flash flood took out a 30-foot bridge over a minor arroyo in Tucson and turned lethal through a bizarre fluke of geography. The rain was so heavy that it laid down a thin sheet of water over the flat desert surrounding the wash,

natural riverbeds, and over dams designed to control them. They are a natural consequence of our geography. A basically arid land punctuated by mountain ranges spiking more than 10,000 feet into the sky is a land of extremes. The mountains blockade inbound weather fronts and turn them into heavy snows or rains. Natural draws in the mountains funnel immense amounts of water into narrow channels, which then deepen with erosion.

The effects are awesome — and humbling. Hikers in slot canyons such as Antelope will nervously eye nests of flotsam — fireplace-sized logs and brush — lodged between the canyon walls 20 to 30 feet overhead, marking the high-water level of some recent flood. In the vast southern Arizona floods of 1993, residents of dozens of towns and cities watched raging water chew off house-sized chunks of banks of normally dry rivers — and, all too often, the houses built on those chunks. The rampage caused $60 million worth of damage.

concealing the fact that the bridge was gone. One by one, cars charged like lemmings into the raging arroyo, where they were promptly swept away. Eleven died before police were able to stop traffic.

In August of 1997, a tower of amber water corkscrewed through Antelope Canyon, one of the twisting, delicately sculptured slot canyons near the Arizona-Utah border, drowning 11 Europeans who were on a guided tour. The fact that floods just like it, distributed over millions of years, are the very thing responsible for the canyon's astounding beauty was no consolation to the victims. "It's just like being caught in a washing machine," said a Navajo policeman investigating the accident. "There's nothing you can do."

The floods come quickly in summer or gather up slowly in winter; they occur in deserts, mountains, and canyons, along

The flood waters look like liquid mud, the intense color of rich, red-brown chocolate: The upper reaches of Soap Creek (above) in the Grand Canyon rush angrily after a September downpour. This flooded side canyon (right) sends storm runoff into the Colorado River.

That 1993 flood did have its moment of comic relief. A Clifton resident was helping evacuate a cousin when the swelling San Francisco River plopped a 45-pound catfish onto the driveway. The fish became another casualty of the flood: When the water receded, the cousins fried it.

Destructive floods, like forest fires, are an unintended consequence of civilization. We encourage them even while we struggle to control them. Every acre of city asphalt is an acre where rainfall can't be absorbed into the ground, so instead it will run off and gather or spill someplace else, adding to the damage.

If it were not for civilization, there wouldn't be any damage. Floods are a natural force, like wind and fire. Nature is no sentimentalist, as Emerson said, so an oak tree uprooted, a deer drowned, simply become nutrients for some needy protoplasm downstream. Rivers choose new routes, life marches on. Only human vanity begs for exceptions — and mourns the losses when, inevitably, the water furies riot. ◈

GARY LADD ▷

Hikers are wary when they enter a slot canyon: Antelope Canyon can surround a hiker with the serenity of a cathedral (left) or trap the unwary as torrents of muddy rainwater rush in (right).

It doesn't even have to be raining at the points where flash floods occur:
Sabino Creek (above) near Tucson is swollen by snowmelt coming from the
Santa Catalina Mountains above. Morning light (right) shows the swirling
waters of Sabino Creek flooding trees on the bank.

RANDY PRENTICE

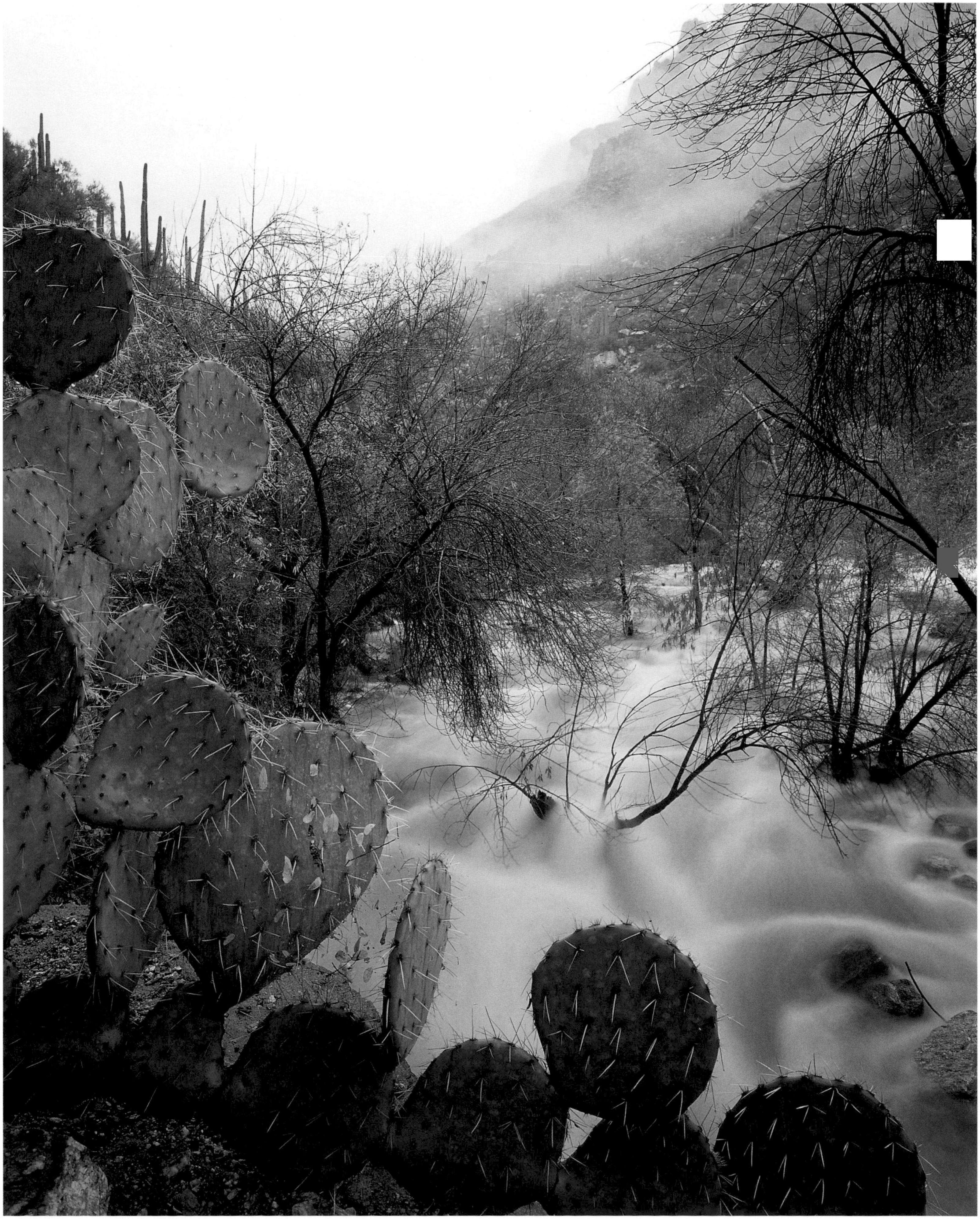

The floods gather up slowly in winter in deserts, mountains, and canyons:
Sabino Creek rushes around sycamore trunks (left) and cottonwood trees
(above) still dressed in winter garb.

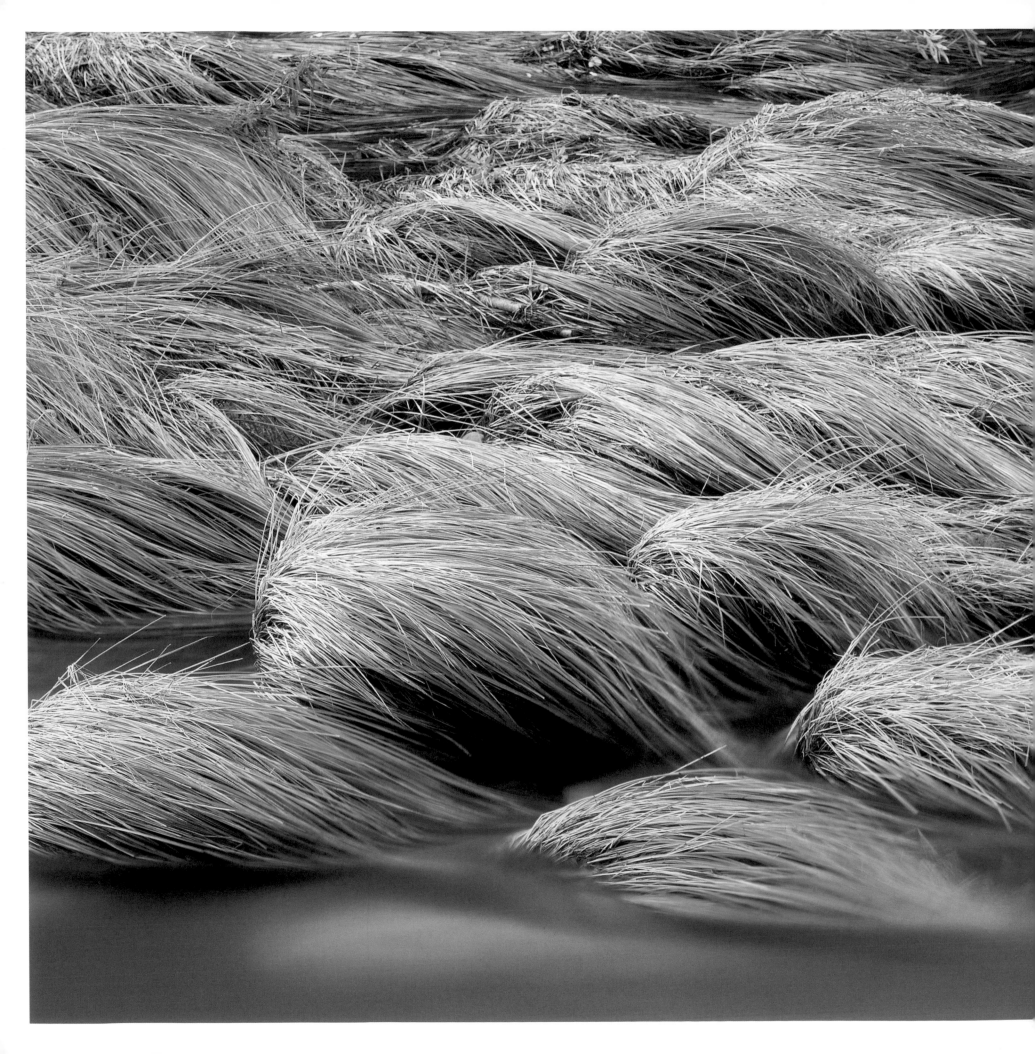

Flooding waterways flatten vegetation along their courses: Tufted grass (left) bears evidence of an August flood on the East Fork of the Black River in the Apache National Forest.

Walls of water dislodge boulders and rocks and bounce them downstream like beachballs: Rocks (above) rest in willow trees along Burro Creek in central Arizona. A monsoon's runoff (right) muscles its way down a drainage in the White Canyon Wilderness south of Superior.

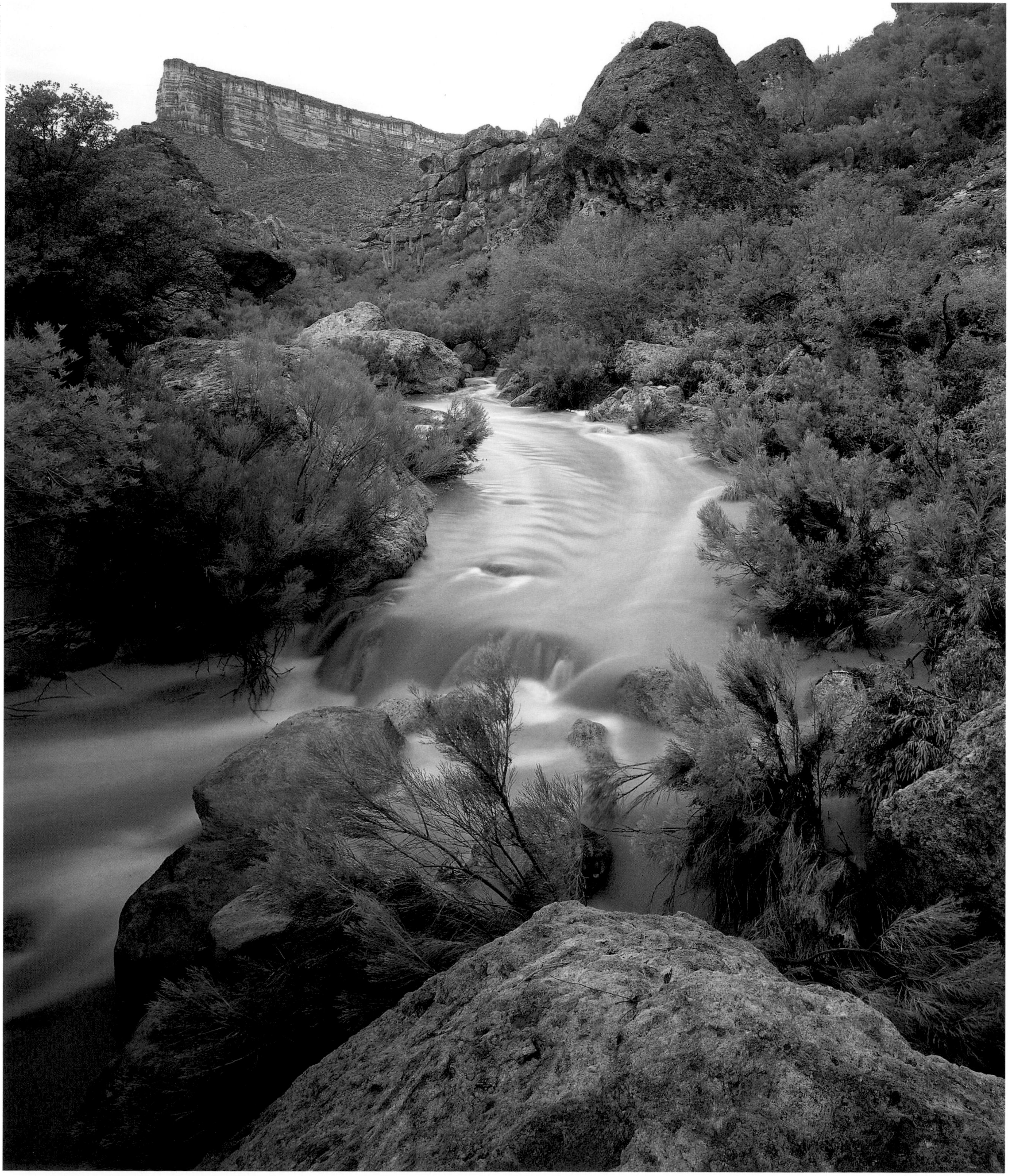

RICHARD K. WEBB

Heavenly Leaves

*As I grow older and conserve my efforts, I shall give this
season my final and undivided attention.*

— Loren Eiseley, "The Secret of Life"

I FIRST SAW THE IMPROBABLE MOUN- tainside mining town of Jerome in October. Even seen from miles away in the Verde Valley, Jerome's spindly Victorian cottages and rooming houses appeared to be embraced by gold-leafed garlands. What a fine coincidence, I thought, for those 19th-century prospectors to have staked their claim where each fall the color of the native foliage would echo the minerals buried in the mountain's depths.

Well, nonsense. Romantic notions about mining towns are always wrong, and this one was no exception. The golden trees were not natives. They were not even wanted. They were *Ailanthus altissima*, the Chinese "tree of heaven," brought in by Phelps Dodge in the 1950s as a quick-growing fix for a landscape that was all but bare after 70 years of the smelter's sulfur dioxide breath. Some years later, after the mining and smelting were long gone, Jerome's residents began to regard the aggressive ailanthus as a scourge, the tree from hell. Still, viewed from a distance they were — and are — gracious ornaments for the town.

The Southwest's fall color is full of surprises like this, unexpected and opportunistic. It isn't like the annual bacchanal back East, where the entire New England forest goes predictably berserk. Arid-land trees have smaller leaves, which conserve transpiration losses, and therefore offer less overt showmanship. They're more subtle, more selective, more varied in their repertoire of effects — and perhaps more of a treat because of all this restraint.

Landscape photographer David Muench always feels a tug toward southeastern Arizona's remote Aravaipa Canyon in the fall, where yellowing sycamores and cottonwoods seem to harvest the sunlight, churn it around in their leaves, and splash it onto the canyon walls as an ethereal amber tint. This reflected light "colors everything it strikes, transforming the whole character of the landscape," Muench says. Indeed it does.

In the sandstone world of Canyon de

In the sandstone world of Canyon de Chelly, giant Frémont cottonwoods form mushroom clouds of brilliant yellow that play spectacularly off the canyon walls: White House Ruin (right), now part of the Canyon de Chelly National Monument, was built by prehistoric people called Anasazi.

Chelly, giant Frémont cottonwoods form mushroom clouds of brilliant yellow that play spectacularly off the red show of the canyon walls. Although cottonwoods are native to the Southwest, these individuals have been planted by the National Park Service since the 1930s to control erosion.

In the countless desert canyons of southern Arizona, sycamores up to 80 feet tall shed their copper leaves into inky pools, where they sail on the increasingly chilly fall breezes. Forget the comic-book renderings of oases with their lonely palms and stagnant ponds; this is the real thing, cool and colorful and wonderfully evocative of the season.

Some of autumn's most incandescent displays occur in the isolated groves of quaking aspen that thrive in the Southwest's coldest climates — elevations of 6,000 to 11,500 feet. Lockett Meadow is the state's premier aspen showroom, a vast crescent of stark white bark and yellow fire backed against the gloomy ponderosa forest and snow cones of the San Francisco Peaks north of Flagstaff. Unlike

Aspens generally huddle exclusively with their own kind, growing in a ghetto that changes color in lockstep: At Lockett Meadow (left and above) in the volcanic inner basin of the San Francisco Peaks north of Flagstaff, slender columns of aspens reach toward the autumn sky.

other deciduous trees, aspens generally huddle exclusively with their own kind, growing in a ghetto that changes color in lockstep, as if a central command center were shutting down their circulatory systems and halting chlorophyll production at precisely the same moment. Which, in a way, is exactly what happens.

Most aspen groves are clonal, meaning that all the trees have reproduced from the root system of a common ancestor and are genetically identical to it. In fact, they all could be considered an *it* — a single plant that responds as a unit to all the variables that affect the timing of each autumn's color: rainfall, temperature, and length of the days.

For sheer variety, Oak Creek Canyon, Zane Grey's "wild, lonely, terrible place," is the unchallenged mecca for Arizona leaf-peepers as, every October, the narrow ribbon of State Route 89A clots with creeping cars. Parking overflows in the choicest spots, most

conspicuously the West Fork of Oak Creek. The canyon's "car-stopper" shrub, as Steve Yoder of The Arboretum at Flagstaff puts it, is the smooth sumac, which bursts into the deepest red of any native species. The hike-stopper — its subtleties are best appreciated on foot — is the bigtooth maple, which blushes through the entire spectrum of pink, vermilion, scarlet, and burgundy, sometimes all on the same tree, all at once.

In 1996, *The New York Times* reported that autumn leaves have become big business in tourism, with quite a few states, Arizona included, actively promoting their color festival. "We've had to struggle to maintain market share," complained Vermont's tourism commissioner. If Nature cared to read the *Times*, she probably would be more than a little annoyed at the commercialization. But happily, this show remains — and it always will — something that can't be controlled, scheduled, packaged, arranged, preserved, or bottled. Or even taxed. ⊠

For sheer variety, Oak Creek Canyon, Zane Grey's "wild, lonely, terrible place," is the unchallenged mecca for Arizona leaf-peepers: Maple trees (right) color a wash in Oak Creek Canyon with gold, orange, and red. Sumac (above) spreads a scarlet tint over a meadow near Pine.

The Southwest's fall color is full of surprises like this, unexpected and opportunistic. It isn't like the annual bacchanal back East: The gaze soars upward (left) to a canopy of quaking aspens in full autumn gold. Aspens (above) in the Roaring Springs area deep in the Grand Canyon stand out against the Canyon's striated walls and buttes.

Arid-land trees are selective in their repertoire of effects — and perhaps more of a treat because of this: Seen from an aspen-covered mountain (left), distant Ship Rock, a Navajo Nation landmark and namesake for a Navajo town, thrusts upward from a broad valley.

Heavenly Leaves | 133

Some of autumn's most incandescent displays occur in the isolated groves of quaking aspen that thrive in the Southwest's coldest climates: Snow (right), blue spruce, and aspens decorate DeMotte Park in the North Kaibab National Forest in the Arizona Strip north of the Grand Canyon. Frost (above) tinges an aspen leaf.

DICK DIETRICH ▷

Stark white bark and yellow fire highlight ponderosa forests: Aspens (left) grow not far from the walls of Tsegi Canyon in Navajo National Monument. Hart Prairie Road (above) near Flagstaff disappears into autumn colors.

MICHAEL COLLIER

Although cottonwoods are native to the Southwest, these trees have been planted by the National Park Service since the 1930s to control erosion: Groves of cottonwoods thrive in rocky canyons near Navajo Mountain (above) and Canyon de Chelly (right).

In the countless desert canyons of southern Arizona, forget the comic-book renderings of oases with their lonely palms and stagnant ponds; this is the real thing: Maples (left) lend their color to the entire landscape in the Chiricahuas. Agave (above) usually pictured in desert scenes grows among maples in the Galiuro Mountains' Ash Creek Canyon.

The Snowman Cometh

Snow fell in the Valley on Wednesday,
but the entire accumulation wasn't enough to put together
a respectable snowman.

— *The Arizona Republic*, February 15, 1990

IT IS A CHILLY, CLOUDY WINTER morning in Phoenix and the Valley of the Sun. Jerry Sieve, a photographer whose work frequently graces *Arizona Highways*, is homesick for snow. Scanning the mountains on the horizon, he spots fresh white tunics on the shoulders of the Mazatzals northeast of Phoenix. Piling into his pickup, he chases the snow line up the foothills, shovels his pickup bed full of the alien stuff, and trucks it back to his house. Working fast, Jerry creates that elusive Sasquatch of the desert, a Phoenix snowman.

Lowland Arizonans run a little crazy when it snows, which is extremely seldom. Tucson, elevation 2,389 feet, gets blanketed with an average of an inch a year. Phoenix, 1,300 feet lower, goes decades without seeing that much. Yuma, 141 feet above sea level, has never seen measurable snow — defined as .01 of an inch — since anyone has been measuring. When snow dusts any of the low desert cities, atrophied slick-road driving skills fail, schools close as if an epidemic were raging, and photographers fan out to catch the desert in a contradiction of itself. A two-armed saguaro in the snow can seem either comic or pathetic, a clown lathered with whipped cream or a waif caught out in a storm.

Fog is nearly as rare, and just as strange in its effects. When winter clouds cruise in low over Sedona and thread themselves through the red rocks, the buttes and monoliths become ghostly icebergs cruising through the sky. If the sun happens to emerge, the light bouncing off the mountains may even color the clouds: red fog. In the mountain canyons of the Sonoran Desert, saguaros appear to march up the canyon walls into gray oblivion, sentinels guarding unearthly mysteries.

These are the aberrations, of course. Tucson's average January low is 38° F and the high is 64°, with fingers of cirrus clouds tentatively stretching across a jewel-blue sky. German-born Father Ignaz Pfefferkorn, the 18th-century Sonoran missionary, allowed himself a moment of smugness when he ob-

He spots fresh white tunics on the shoulders of the Mazatzal Mountains northeast of Phoenix: Snow dusts the Four Peaks (above) in the Mazatzals while the desert below basks in balmy weather.

Nearly as rare as snow, and just as strange in its effects: Fog (right) drapes the mountains behind upper Sabino Canyon north of Tucson.

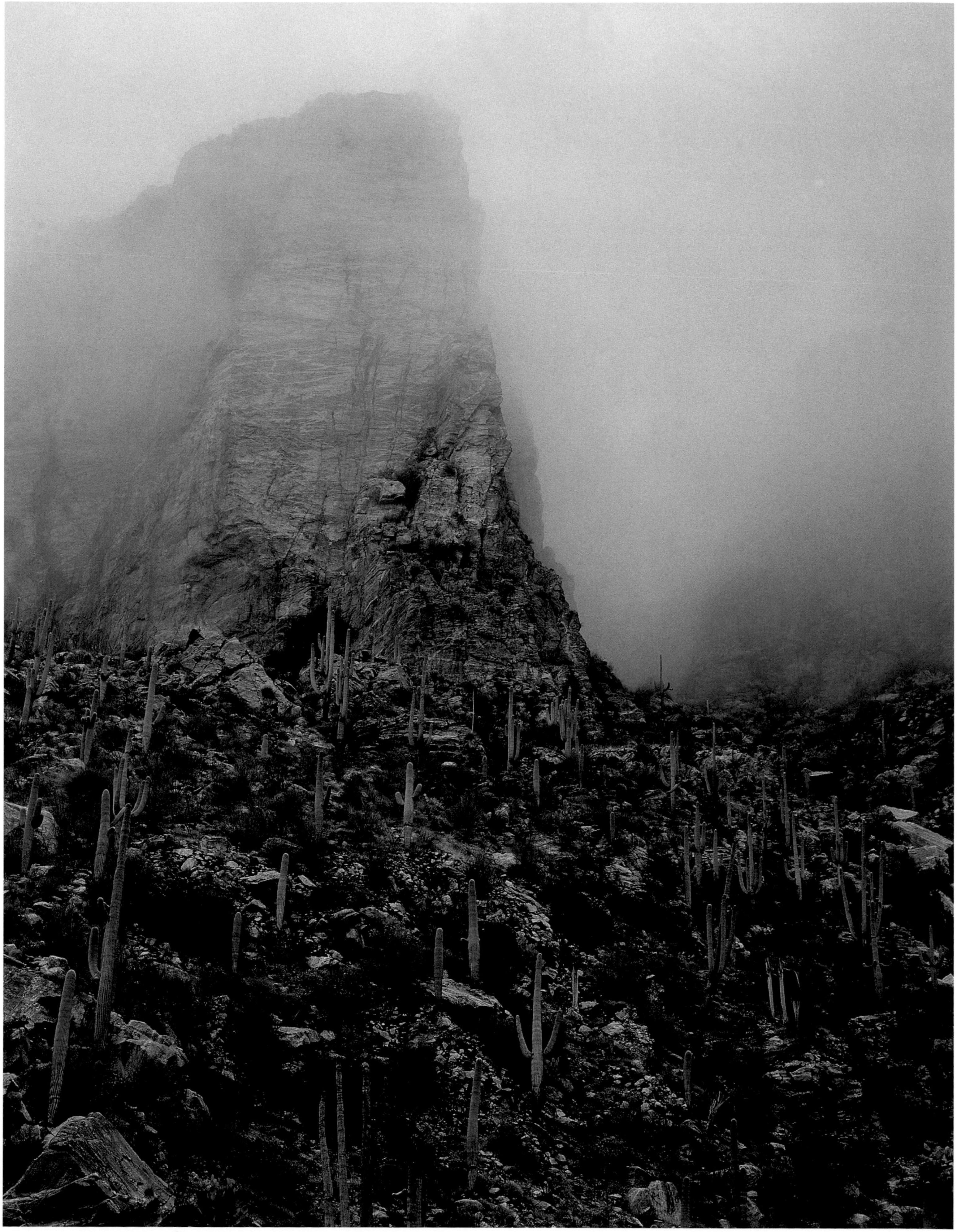

DAVID W. LAZAROFF

served that the tender natives had to build fires to keep warm through these benign winters. "A German," he bragged, "needs nothing more than a good mantle to protect himself sufficiently against the cold . . ."

Pfefferkorn didn't exactly sound homesick when writing those sunny lines, but had he wanted snow, all he would have needed to do was climb a nearby mountain and wait for the next Pacific front. Our mountains entertain winter — real winter, with blizzard-force wind and waist-deep snow — sporadically but convincingly. Flagstaff, at 6,905 feet, is the snowiest metropolitan area in the country: Its 109-inch annual average beats Syracuse, New York, by four inches. In compensation, the snow doesn't hang around forever. In the Colorado Plateau's semi-arid climate, snow actually *evaporates* at up to 3 inches a day.

Arizona mountains entertain real winter, with blizzard-force wind and waist-deep snow: Pine tree limbs (right) droop from the weight of snow while golden aspens spark the icy scene at the base of the San Francisco Peaks. Snow (above) clings to fans of pine needles after a storm on the Mogollon Rim.

"The first two or three feet are a lot of fun," Platt Cline wrote in *The Sheriff Magazine* of April 1949, soon after Flagstaff tunneled out from a record 11 feet between December 22, 1948 and January 22, 1949. Then the party stopped. Houses collapsed. Trucks hauling fuel oil were stranded. People couldn't get medical help, and doctors couldn't make house calls. "It wasn't fun any more," Cline wrote, "but deadly, dangerously serious business."

Arizona has complex relationships with winter. Blizzards raking across the remote, red mesas of the Navajo Nation can bring real misery; in 1987, the Arizona National Guard had to airlift tons of food and hay to stranded farmers and sheep. Yet just to the south, the White Mountain Apaches depend on the same storm systems for their economy. If these mountains get at least a 30-inch snow base by Christmas, the tribe's Sunrise Ski Resort will be packed with 8,000 to 10,000 bodies a day for the holiday season. Snow can make the Grand Canyon inaccessible (the North Rim, in fact, closes from mid-October to mid-May), but it also renders it achingly beautiful — "a delicious layered cake with tons of frosting," as Canyon observer Sjors Horstman described it. Winter, in this country, has an endless supply of disguises — and personalities.

Phoenix has ballooned into America's sixth-largest city in large part because it has no winter, but its life depends on what happens up in snowman country — the 13,000 square miles of mountain and plateau that form the watersheds of the Salt and Verde rivers. Each winter, snow surveyors for the Salt River Project or the U.S. Department of Agriculture ski around to test sites and measure the snowpack's depth and water content. The information helps them predict runoff into the rivers and manage the reservoirs that furnish up to half of metropolitan Phoenix's water. Phoenix owes its existence to snow — a delicious irony that never occurs to anyone on a sunny, 75° January day. ⌗

Phoenix owes its existence to snow: A wash (right) begins to fill with snow runoff in February in the Mazatzal Mountains near Sunflower. The water could end up in a metropolitan Phoenix home.

In fog, buttes and monoliths become ghostly icebergs: Along the North Kaibab Trail (above) a craggy juniper seems intensely green against gray-shrouded limestone spires in the Grand Canyon.

DAVID MUENCH ▷

A saguaro in the snow can seem either comic or pathetic, a clown lathered with whipped cream or a waif caught out in a storm: Snowy desert brush and saguaros (left) wreath the foggy cliffs of Finger Rock Canyon near Tucson. Snow and fog (above) wash out desert colors, leaving a ghostly cast.

Blizzards raking across the remote Navajo Nation can leave scenic trails and, perhaps, problems for the area's residents: The reservation's Honeymoon Arch (above) and Monument Valley (right) contrast with winter snow.

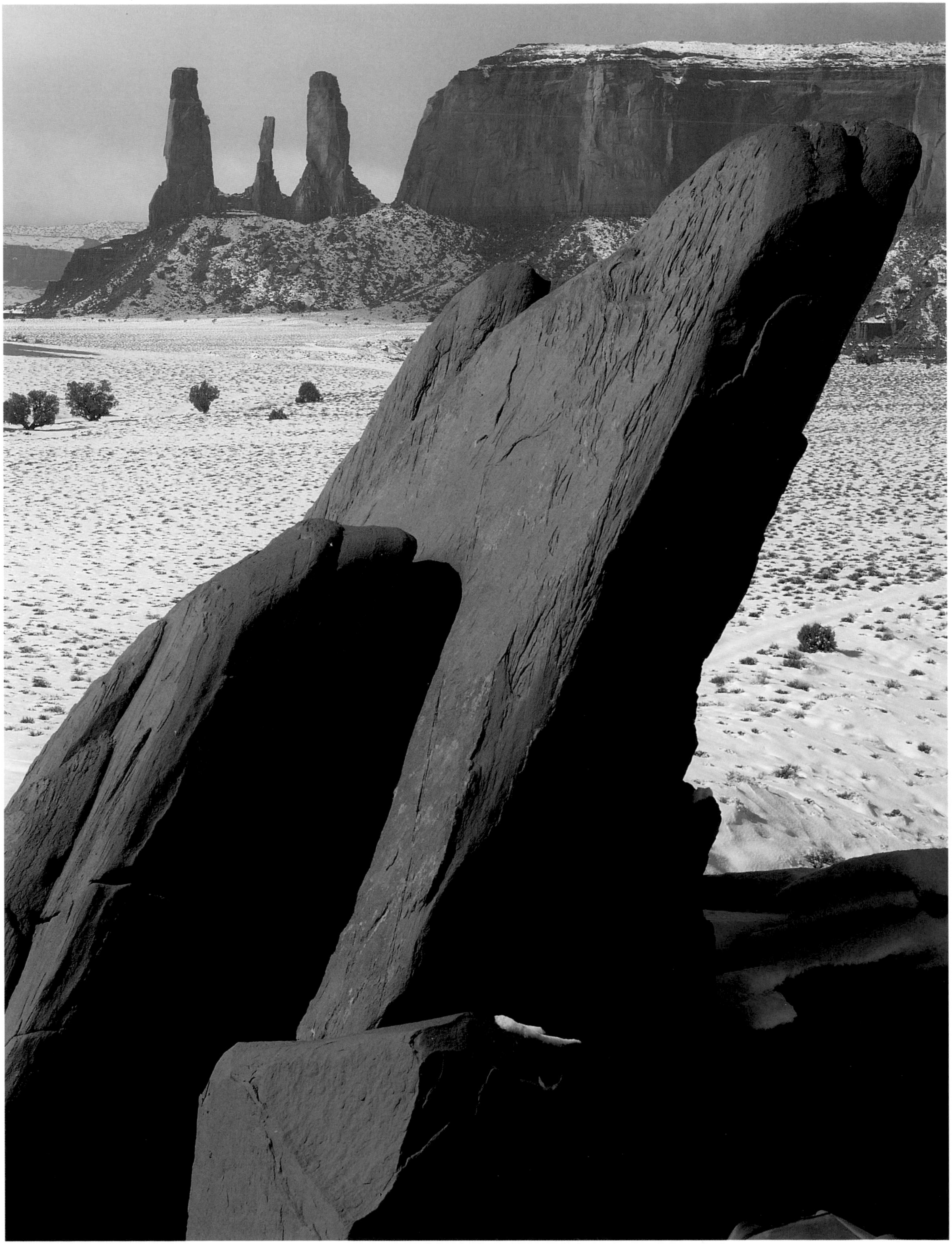

DAVID MUENCH

Winter clouds cruise in low, threading through the red rocks: The Mogollon Rim (left), as seen from Schnebly Hill Road east of Sedona, catches a dusting of snow.

RANDY PRENTICE ▷

In the Colorado Plateau's semi-arid climate, snow evaporates at up to 3 inches a day: Pine forests (left and above) camouflage the fact that they exist in a semi-arid environment.

Flagstaff, at 6,905 feet, is the snowiest metropolitan area in the country: The San Francisco Peaks (above and right) catch much of the snow in the Flagstaff area.

TOM TILL

Did the Anasazi make snowmen? Perhaps children who lived in what
now is called the White House Ruin (above) in Canyon de Chelly
frolicked in the snow.